Boston

Let It Begin Here!

LEXINGTON & CONCORD
First Battles of the American Revolution

DENNIS BRINDELL FRADIN

Illustrations by LARRY DAY

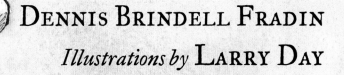

WALKER & COMPANY ✸ NEW YORK

Who's Who

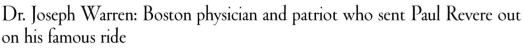 ## American Side

 Samuel Adams: Boston Tea Party organizer and public enemy number 1 to the British

Colonel James Barrett: Concord militia commander

 Prince Estabrook: African American slave who fought and was wounded at the Battle of Lexington

John Hancock: Popular Massachusetts politician who was public enemy number 2 to the British

 Captain John Parker: Leader of the Lexington militia

Paul Revere: Boston silversmith and messenger for the Massachusetts patriots

Dr. Joseph Warren: Boston physician and patriot who sent Paul Revere out on his famous ride

 ## British Side

 General Thomas Gage: Royal governor of Massachusetts and commander in chief of British troops in North America

 George III: King of Great Britain

 Major John Pitcairn: Leader of the British advance party that fought at Lexington

 Lieutenant Colonel Francis Smith: Leader of the British expedition sent by Gage to Lexington and Concord

Side Unknown

 Margaret Kemble Gage: General Gage's American wife, who may have secretly informed the Americans of British plans

Introduction

Virginia, the first of England's 13 American colonies, was settled in 1607. Americans accepted English rule for about 160 years.

When England began taxing the colonists in the 1760s, Americans protested, most violently in Massachusetts. On December 16, 1773, a mob directed by Samuel Adams destroyed British tea in Boston Harbor during an incident known as the Boston Tea Party. Three months later, in March 1774, John Hancock of Boston proposed that the colonies break free from Britain and become the United States of America. Across the colonies, local militias (emergency troops) prepared for possible war with England.

On April 14, 1775, General Thomas Gage, royal governor of Massachusetts, received secret orders. British leaders, including King George III, wanted him to strike at the Massachusetts rebels. Gage sent out a 700-man army under Lieutenant Colonel Francis Smith on the night of April 18. The troops were to arrest Samuel Adams and John Hancock in Lexington, Massachusetts, then destroy American military supplies at nearby Concord. The colonists were cowards who would "run away" from a fight, predicted one of Gage's officers, Major John Pitcairn. Americans themselves weren't so sure that they could face up to the mighty British army.

APRIL 18, 1775, 9:30 P.M. Paul Revere, a Boston silversmith and
messenger for the patriots, receives an urgent request to visit Dr. Joseph
Warren's home. Upon Paul's arrival, Dr. Warren assigns him a double
mission. He must warn Samuel Adams and John Hancock in Lexington,
and then the patriots in Concord, that the British are coming.

How does Dr. Warren know that the British plan to invade Lexington and Concord? General Gage's American wife may have told him. Margaret Kemble Gage, who is from New Jersey, opposes any action that might hurt her native country, and may have betrayed her husband's scheme.

APRIL 18, 1775, 10:00 P.M. Before leaving Boston, Revere stops by a friend's house and tells him, "Two lanterns!" The friend hangs two lanterns in the steeple of the Old North Church, signaling patriots in the area that the British are leaving Boston by boat before marching inland. Were the British leaving by land, Paul would have ordered one lantern placed in the steeple.

Paul sets out on his journey from Boston to Lexington. The nearly full moon lights the way as two friends row Paul across the Charles River to Charlestown. There the 40-year-old silversmith borrows a fast horse named Brown Beauty and begins the 13-mile ride to Lexington.

Near Cambridge, two British officers suddenly bolt out from behind a huge tree and try to capture Paul. Brown Beauty is too fast for them, though, and Paul is too skilled a rider. He guides the powerful mare onto another road. The two officers chase him, but they are soon left far behind.

On he gallops, warning people along the way that the British are coming.

APRIL 19, 1775, 12:00 A.M. Paul reaches Lexington and bangs on the door of the house where Hancock and Adams are staying. Guards outside the house tell Paul to stop making so much noise. "Noise!" yells Paul. "You'll have noise enough before long! The regulars are coming out!" *Regulars, redcoats,* and *lobsterbacks* are what the Americans call the British troops.

Adams and Hancock are now awake. "Let him in!" Hancock tells the guards.

Thanks to Revere's warning, Adams and Hancock flee by carriage. Meanwhile, a bell is rung to call Lexington's militiamen to arms.

APRIL 19, 1775, 1:00 A.M. Having completed half his mission, Paul Revere heads for Concord. Along the way, he meets Dr. Samuel Prescott, who is riding home after visiting his fiancée. Prescott offers to help spread the alarm to Concord. This proves to be a stroke of luck.

Paul Revere never gets to Concord, for British troops block

his way. But Prescott jumps his horse over a stone wall to elude the redcoats. The young doctor rides through woods and swampland and enters Concord by 2:00 in the morning.

Following Dr. Prescott's warning, Concord's alarm is sounded. As the bell tolls, townspeople hide military supplies in barns and homes, and Concord's militiamen prepare to fight.

APRIL 19, 1775, ABOUT 5:00 A.M. The men of Lexington have been waiting more than four hours for the redcoats. Finally, near sunrise, a lookout gallops into Lexington, shouting, "The lobsterbacks are down the road!"

Within minutes, about 70 Lexington militiamen gather on Lexington Green, summoned by the town drummer. Instead of uniforms, the men on the field wear farm clothes. Instead of army weapons, they carry old hunting muskets. Some are teenagers, like the 19-year-old drummer William Diamond. Others, such as 62-year-old Robert Munroe, are rather old to fight. There are several pairs of fathers and sons. One soldier, Prince Estabrook, is a slave who has been promised his freedom if he helps fight the British.

The men awaiting the British have one thing in common. They are scared, for they are about to face an army from the world's strongest nation.

"Stand your ground," the leader of the Lexington militia, Captain John Parker, reportedly tells his men. "Don't fire unless fired upon. But if they mean to have a war, let it begin here!"

At about 5:20 in the morning an advance party led by Major John Pitcairn—the officer who boasted that the Americans would run away—approaches Lexington Green.

"Disperse, ye rebels, disperse in the name of the king!" Pitcairn yells at the Americans. "Lay down your arms!"

Facing the guns of several hundred redcoats, Captain Parker decides to back down. He tells his men to go home but to remain armed. Most of the men start walking away. A few don't. Captain Parker's cousin Jonas Parker, a grandfather who has vowed never to flee from the British, stands his ground. So does 62-year-old Robert Munroe.

Suddenly a shot rings out—from which side is unknown.
Moments later the redcoats let loose a torrent of gunfire. Robert
Munroe is shot to death where he stands. Jonas Parker is wounded
but, true to his vow, fires his musket from the ground until killed by
a bayonet thrust. Jonathan Harrington, walking home, is shot near
his doorstep. He crawls a few yards and dies in front of his horrified
wife and son.

The Battle of Lexington lasts just ten minutes. In all, eight

Americans die and ten are wounded in this first battle of the
Revolutionary War. Several Americans have returned enemy fire,
wounding Major Pitcairn in the finger and another British soldier in
the leg.

Following the battle, the entire British force meets up and heads
to Concord, five miles to the west. They expect that most of the
Americans will "run away" there, too.

APRIL 19, 1775, 7:00 A.M. Ninety minutes after the
Lexington battle, Lieutenant Colonel Francis Smith leads his full
force of 700 redcoats into Concord. There, the several hundred
troops commanded by 65-year-old Colonel James Barrett are as
terrified as the Lexington men had been.

One . . . two . . . then three hours pass. The Americans only stand and watch as the sea of redcoats takes over their town, seizing weapons and gunpowder.

APRIL 19, 1775, ABOUT 10:00 A.M. A cloud of smoke from fires the British have set rises over Concord. The smoke above their town stirs something in the Americans' hearts. "Will you let them burn the town down?" one man asks Colonel Barrett.

Colonel Barrett orders his troops to advance toward 100 redcoats guarding Concord's North Bridge. The Americans are about 200 feet away when the British fire at them. Two Americans are killed and several are wounded, but this time the Americans don't run.

"Fire, fellow soldiers, for God's sake, *fire!*" shouts an American officer.

"*Fire!*" "*Fire!*" "*Fire!*" "*Fire!*" "*Fire!*" the Americans along the bridge yell.

The Americans open fire, killing or wounding about 15 redcoats. Astonished that the colonists have fought back, and seeing more Americans pouring into Concord, the whole British force begins retreating toward Boston.

But the Americans aren't finished. They pursue the redcoats, shooting at them from behind trees and stone walls. News of the American defeat at Lexington has spread, and militia units pour in from far and wide seeking revenge. "It seemed as if men came down from the clouds," a British survivor later writes. About 3,600 patriots from 40 towns join the fight, turning the road into a 20-mile-long battlefield.

Near Lexington, a group of Americans with a special score to settle—Captain John Parker and his remaining men—lie in wait. One of them takes aim at the British leader, Lieutenant Colonel Smith, and wounds him.

Some of the fiercest fighting occurs at the town of Menotomy. There a group of redcoats rushes 78-year-old Samuel Whittemore as he fires at them from behind a stone wall.

Whittemore brings down three redcoats before the British shoot him in the head and stab him 13 times with bayonets. Amazingly, he survives, and lives to the age of 96.

APRIL 19, 1775, 7:00 P.M.

The British finally limp into the Boston area. They have suffered a devastating defeat. Nearly 300 redcoats have been killed or wounded. The colonists have suffered about 100 casualties at the running Battle of Concord—the first American triumph of the Revolutionary War.

Afterword

The Battles of Lexington and Concord did more than begin the Revolutionary War. They showed England and the rest of the world that Americans would fight for their freedom. The battles were also bloody reminders that achieving independence would cost many lives.

Winning the war took eight years. Finally, on September 3, 1783, the United States and Britain signed the Treaty of Paris. Britain recognized the independence of the United States, ending the war that had begun one spring morning at Lexington and Concord.

What Happened to the People

 AMERICAN SIDE

Samuel Adams: Remembered as "the Father of American Independence," he was also the governor of Massachusetts from 1793 to 1797

Colonel James Barrett: Died suddenly on April 11, 1779—four years after the Battle of Concord—at the age of 69

Prince Estabrook: Freed following his Revolutionary War service

John Hancock: Elected first Massachusetts state governor in 1780, he held his state's highest office for a total of 11 years

Captain John Parker: Was ill with tuberculosis at the time of the Battle of Lexington and died five months later at the age of 46

Paul Revere: Had 16 children, and by the time of his death at age 83, more than 50 grandchildren

Dr. Joseph Warren: Was killed at the age of 34 at the Battle of Bunker Hill in what is now Boston

BRITISH SIDE

General Thomas Gage: The Battles of Lexington and Concord—and Bunker Hill in June 1775—hurt his military reputation; in the fall of 1775 he left for England, where he died in 1787

George III: Afflicted with a condition that caused bouts of mental illness, the king lived for nearly 40 years after losing his American colonies, dying in 1820 at the age of 81

Major John Pitcairn: Was killed two months later at the Battle of Bunker Hill

Lieutenant Colonel Francis Smith: Received much of the blame for events at Concord; later he did poorly at other campaigns

SIDE UNKNOWN

Margaret Kemble Gage: Sent to England by her husband, General Thomas Gage, soon after the Battles of Lexington and Concord, she endured an unhappy marriage until his death in 1787; she died in England at age 90, never having revealed whether she had betrayed her husband's military plan

Sources

Fischer, David Hackett. *Paul Revere's Ride*. New York: Oxford University Press, 1994.

Fleming, Thomas. *The First Stroke: Lexington, Concord, and the Beginning of the American Revolution*. Washington, D.C.: National Park Service, 1978.

French, Allen. *The Day of Concord and Lexington*. Boston: Little, Brown, 1925.

Frothingham, Richard. *History of the Siege of Boston, and of the Battles of Lexington, Concord, and Bunker Hill*. 3rd ed. Boston: Little, Brown, 1872.

Galvin, John R. *The Minute Men: The First Fight*. 2nd ed., rev. Washington, D.C.: Pergamon-Brassey's, 1989.

Tourtellot, Arthur Bernon. *William Diamond's Drum: The Beginning of the War of the American Revolution*. Garden City, New York: Doubleday, 1959.

For Further Reading

Johnson, Neil. *The Battle of Lexington and Concord*. New York: Four Winds, 1992.

Kent, Deborah. *Lexington and Concord*. New York: Children's Press, 1997.

King, David. *Lexington and Concord*. New York: Twenty-First Century, 1997.

Krensky, Stephen. *Paul Revere's Midnight Ride*. New York: HarperCollins, 2002.

Nordstrom, Judy. *Concord and Lexington*. New York: Dillon, 1993.

Peacock, Judith. *The Battles of Lexington and Concord*. Mankato, MN: Bridgestone Books, 2002.

Whitelaw, Nancy. *The Shot Heard Round the World: The Battles of Lexington and Concord*. Greensboro, NC: Morgan Reynolds, 2001.

First published in the United States of America in 2005 by Walker Publishing Company, Inc.

Published simultaneously in Canada by Fitzhenry and Whiteside, Markham, Ontario L3R 4T8

For information about permission to reproduce selections from this book, write to Permissions, Walker & Company, 104 Fifth Avenue, New York, New York, 10011

Library of Congress Cataloging-in-Publication Data

Fradin, Dennis B.
    Let it begin here! : Lexington & Concord : first battles of the American Revolution / Dennis Brindell Fradin ; illustrations by Larry Day.
        p. cm.
    Includes bibliographical references.
    ISBN 0-8027-8945-5 — ISBN 0-8027-8946-3
1. Lexington, Battle of, Lexington, Mass., 1775—Juvenile literature. 2. Concord, Battle of, Concord, Mass., 1775—Juvenile literature. I. Day, Larry, 1956- ill. II. Title.

E241.L6F75 2005
973.3'311—dc22

2004049473

The illustrations for this book were created using pen and ink with watercolor and gouache on watercolor paper.

Book design by Nicole Gastonguay

Visit Walker & Company's Web site at
www.walkeryoungreaders.com

Printed in Hong Kong

10 9 8 7 6 5 4 3 2 1 0

New
Hampshire

Massachusetts

New York

Concord
Lexington

Boston

Rhode Island

Connecticut

Pennsylvania

New Jersey

Delaware

Virginia

Maryland

North Carolina

South
Carolina

Georgia

The Thirteen Colonies
1775

For Miss Anna Rose Fradin,
for whom everything is just beginning. —D. B. F

For my mother and father, for their rebellious nature. —L. D.